We Need HONEYBEES

RYAN NAGELHOUT

PowerKiDS
press.

New York

Published in 2016 by The Rosen Publishing Group, Inc.
29 East 21st Street, New York, NY 10010

First Edition

Editor: Caitie McAneney
Book Design: Mickey Harmon

Photo Credits: Cover (image) szefei/Shutterstock.com; cover, pp. 1, 3, 4, 6, 8, 11, 16–18, 21–24 (background) Click Bestsellers/Shutterstock.com; p. 5 (wasp) schankz/Shutterstock.com; p. 5 (honeybee) Dancestrokes/Shutterstock.com; pp. 6 (queen bee), 7 (drone) Frank Greenaway/Dorling Kindersley/Getty Images; p. 7 (worker bees) Darios/Shutterstock.com; p. 8 grafvision/Shutterstock.com; p. 10 Kippy Spilker/Shutterstock.com; pp. 12–13 l i g h t p o e t/Shutterstock.com; pp. 14–15 Warut Prathaksithorn/Shutterstock.com; p. 16 Nataly Karol/Shutterstock.com; p. 17 Tyler Olson/Shutterstock.com; p. 19 Natalie Behring/Stringer/Getty Images; p. 20 Thomas Lohnes/Contributor/Getty Images News/Getty Images; p. 22 (hive) PCHT/Shutterstock.com; p. 22 (flower) Guy Zidel/Shutterstock.com; p. 22 (bees) Protasov AN/Shutterstock.com.

Library of Congress Cataloging-in-Publication Data

Nagelhout, Ryan, author.
We need honeybees / Ryan Nagelhout.
    pages cm. — (Creatures we can't live without)
Includes bibliographical references and index.
ISBN 978-1-4994-0981-9 (pbk.)
ISBN 978-1-4994-1024-2 (6 pack)
ISBN 978-1-4994-1039-6 (library binding)
1. Honeybee—Juvenile literature. I. Title. II. Series: Creatures we can't live without.
QL568.A6N34 2015
595.79'9—dc23

                              2015006113

Manufactured in the United States of America

CPSIA Compliance Information: Batch #WS15PK: For Further Information contact Rosen Publishing, New York, New York at 1-800-237-9932

CONTENTS

HARDWORKING HONEYBEES

No one likes getting stung by a bee. When you see a bee outside, it's best to stay out of its way. You might think bees are scary, but did you know we need them? Honeybees are important for making food—and not just honey. In fact, they help all kinds of plants grow, from avocados to almonds. Hardworking honeybees are important parts of their **ecosystems**.

Unfortunately, honeybee populations are decreasing in some places. That's why it's important to know how they help and what's happening to them. Let's find out why we need honeybees!

CREATURE CLUE

There are seven different kinds of true honeybees, but some honey wasps and bumblebees also make small amounts of honey.

HONEYBEE

WASP

You might mistake honeybees for other buzzing yellow and black bugs such as wasps and hornets.

A COLONY OF BEES

Honeybees are flying bugs that live in hives. They build these hives, also called combs, out of wax. They live in groups called swarms or colonies. Bees work together to take care of the hive, find food, and **mate** to keep the colony going. They also work together to survive cold winters.

Each hive has three types of honeybees. The first are the bees we see outside of the nest—female worker bees. Male bees are called drones, and their job is to mate with the queen. The most important bee is the queen bee, which lives inside the nest year-round and lays eggs.

QUEEN BEE

CREATURE CLUE

All worker honeybees are female, but they don't have the parts needed to mate with drones. However, a worker bee **larva** can be turned into a queen bee, which would be able to mate.

WORKER BEES

DRONE

In the winter months, the drones are forced to leave the colony so there will be enough food for the worker bees and larvae, which become new honeybees when spring arrives.

THE QUEEN BEE

The queen honeybee is the only female that mates with drones. The queen then lays eggs to make new honeybees. A hive can have a few hundred drones in it during warm seasons. The queen mates with drones from other hives.

A queen can live up to five years and lay more than 2,000 eggs a day! There's only one queen per hive. When a queen dies, a worker bee larva is fed special food called "royal jelly" that helps the larva become the new queen. A diet of royal jelly makes a queen bee grow to twice the size of a normal honeybee.

CREATURE CLUE

Royal jelly may have some benefits for humans. Scientists are studying how royal jelly can help our kidneys, blood sugar, and blood pressure.

QUEEN BEE

Some scientists believe royal jelly may be
able to fight some kinds of cancer in humans.
However, some people are very **allergic** to
royal jelly, so doctors have to be careful.

Worker honeybees do a dance to tell other workers where to find nectar and pollen. This "waggle" tells bees where the flower is, how far away it is, and how rich the source is.

POLLEN SAC

DOING THE WORK

Some worker honeybees build the hive and keep it clean. Other worker honeybees leave the hive in search of pollen. Honeybees have lots of hairs on their body, which pollen sticks to. The pollen collects in an area on the bee's body called a pollen basket. Then, it's pressed into pollen sacs, which is how the honeybees carry it back to the hive.

When honeybees collect pollen, they also look for nectar. They store this nectar in a "honey stomach," also called a crop. When honeybees come back to the hive, they give their nectar to other worker bees in the hive called processor bees.

CREATURE CLUE

Processor bees put the nectar into honeycombs and add an **enzyme** to help it break down. Next, they use their wings to fan air over the nectar to remove water. This is how it becomes honey!

HELPFUL HONEY

Humans have been eating honey for thousands of years. The taste and color can be very different depending on what flower nectar the honeybees use and where they live. Honey is sweet and makes food taste good. It can be used for cooking and baking. Some people even add it to their drinks!

People have long thought honey has healing powers. Ancient Egyptians mixed honey with other elements to make **medicine**. The Greek thinker Aristotle (384 BC to 322 BC) mentioned the healing benefits of honey in his writings. Honey has special qualities that can help kill germs and heal wounds and burns.

CREATURE CLUE

Eating local honey might help people who are allergic to things in their surroundings.

Nectar is about 80 percent water, while honey is less than 19 percent water when it's finished.

Cross-pollination is important in creating **biodiversity** in ecosystems because it makes new plants grow.

FRUITS OF LABOR

Honeybees provide us with honey, but they also help many kinds of plants to grow. On their search for pollen, honeybees move between different plants. When they land on plants, some of the pollen they've collected is left on the plant. The movement of pollen from plant to plant is called cross-pollination and helps different plants create fruit.

More than 30 percent of the world's crops and 90 percent of wild plants need cross-pollination to survive. Many of the fruits, vegetables, and nuts we eat—such as almonds, apples, carrots, and avocados—need honeybees to cross-pollinate their flowers and help them grow.

CREATURE CLUE

Honeybees aren't the only animals that cross-pollinate. Bats, butterflies, and hummingbirds also help plants through cross-pollination.

FARMING BEES

Many honeybees live in the wild, but some are raised on farms. Beekeepers, people who take care of bees, help honeybees make hives in movable wooden boxes. They keep the bees healthy and collect their honey and wax to sell. Beekeepers often keep their bees in **orchards** and near plants they want cross-pollinated.

Some people keep bees near their garden to help their plants grow!

Beekeeping is a big business all over the world. In the United States alone, bees cross-pollinate more than $15 billion in crops per year. Honeybee honey also makes farmers more than $150 million per year. Many people are worried about honeybees disappearing because without cross-pollination, we might run low on food.

CREATURE CLUE

Almond growers in California bring honeybees in from other states to grow their crop. About half of all honeybees in the United States are used to make $2.3 billion of almonds each year.

COLONY CRISIS

In 2006, beekeepers in the United States say something strange happened. Many of their honeybees suddenly left their hives and never came back. The bees appeared to be healthy before they left. Scientists called this strange disappearance "colony collapse disorder." But what's causing it?

Scientists think **climate change** may have changed the time of year some flowers bloom. They also think the loss of honeybee **habitats** and the use of **pesticides** that kill bees play a part. No one knows for sure what's causing the bees to leave, but honeybee populations may continue to drop every year.

CREATURE CLUE

Honeybees can live in many different kinds of habitats, but they prefer to live where there are many flowering plants. Unfortunately, when a meadow is replaced with new houses, the local bee colonies may suffer.

Many scientists are researching bees to understand why they leave their hives.

Some beekeepers are taking care of bees in urban areas such as on top of buildings.

HOW TO HELP

We now know that honeybees help us by cross-pollinating fruit, vegetables, and nuts. They also provide delicious honey they make on their own. Even though they may sting, honeybees play an important role in what we eat.

Farmers and scientists are working hard to help save honeybees, and you can help, too. Make sure the pesticides your family uses don't hurt honeybees, or don't use pesticides at all. You can also ask your family to keep honeybees around to help your own garden grow. The next time you see a honeybee outside, remember how important it is to your next meal!

CREATURE CLUE

There are many natural ways to keep pests away without using harmful chemicals. Some farmers and gardeners bring in helpful bugs to eat the pests.

Things Honeybees Give Us

Whether in the hive or flying flower to flower, honeybees help produce many of the foods we eat everyday.

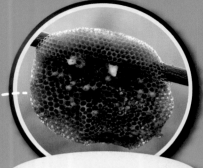

HIVE

HONEY

BEESWAX

FLOWER

APPLES

PEPPERS

ORANGES

LIMES

LEMONS

ALMONDS

GLOSSARY

allergic: Having a bad bodily reaction to certain foods, animals, or surroundings.

biodiversity: The different kinds of life in a place shown by numbers of different kinds of plants and animals.

climate change: Long-term change in Earth's weather, caused partly by human activities such as burning oil and natural gas.

ecosystem: All the living things in an area.

enzyme: A protein made in the body that helps chemical reactions occur.

habitat: The natural home for plants, animals, and other living things.

larva: A bug in an early life stage that has a wormlike form. The plural form is "larvae."

mate: To come together to make babies.

medicine: A drug taken to make a sick person well.

orchard: A place where fruit or nut trees are grown.

pesticide: A chemical used to kill bugs.

INDEX

WEBSITES

Due to the changing nature of Internet links, PowerKids Press has developed an online list of websites related to the subject of this book. This site is updated regularly. Please use this link to access the list: www.powerkidslinks.com/cwcl/bee